DEEP-SEA FISHING

DEEP-SEA FISHING

ODYSSEYS

JIM WHITING

CREATIVE EDUCATION

Published by Creative Education
P.O. Box 227, Mankato, Minnesota 56002
Creative Education is an imprint of The Creative Company
www.thecreativecompany.us

Design by Blue Design (www.bluedes.com)
Production by Joe Kahnke
Art direction by Rita Marshall
Printed in China

Photographs by Alamy (AF archive, Mark Conlin, Deco,
INTERFOTO, National Geographic Creative, Photos 12, Pictorial
Press Ltd, Quagga Media, RosaIreneBetancourt 4), Creative
Commons Wikimedia (U.S. National Archives and Records
Administration), Flickr (Joe Haupt), Getty Images (Bettmann,
John Kuczala, Ronald C. Modra/Sports Imagery), iStockphoto
(Robert Ingelhart, NCHANT, Paul Velgos, wbritten),
Shutterstock (ARENA Creative, Steve Bower, dasytnik, keruko,
Dudarev Mikhail, Suwan Wanawattanawong)

Library of Congress Cataloging-in-Publication Data
Names: Whiting, Jim, author.
Title: Deep-sea fishing / Jim Whiting.
Series: Odysseys in outdoor adventures.
Includes bibliographical references, webography, and index.
Summary: An in-depth survey of the history of deep-sea
fishing, as well as tips and advice on how to prepare for a trip,
and the skills and supplies necessary for an outing on open
water.
Identifiers: LCCN 2016031802 / ISBN 978-1-60818-687-7
(hardcover) / ISBN 978-1-56660-723-0 (eBook)

Subjects: LCSH: Big game fishing—Juvenile literature.
Classification: LCC SH457.5.W554 2017 / DDC 799.16—dc23

CCSS: RI.7.1, 2, 3, 4, 5; RI.8.1, 2, 3, 4, 5; RI.9-10.1, 2, 3, 4; RI.11-12.1,
2, 3, 4; RH.6-8.1, 2, 4, 5; RH.9-10.2, 4, 5

First Edition 9 8 7 6 5 4 3 2 1

CONTENTS

Introduction

Adventure awaits! It's a call from Mother Nature heard by nature lovers and thrill seekers alike. This temptation beckons them, prompting them to pack their gear, pull on their jackets, and head out the door. From mountain peaks to ocean depths and everywhere in between, the earth is a giant playground for those who love to explore and challenge themselves. Not content to follow the beaten

OPPOSITE: On ocean beaches, surf fishing is popular among experienced anglers. Surf fishing rods are typically 12 to 16 feet (3.7–4.9 m) long and often require two hands to cast a baited line farther out in the water. Rod holders or surf spikes can be used to hold rods in the sand.

path, they push the limits by venturing farther, faster, deeper, and higher. Going to such lengths, they discover satisfaction, excitement, and fun. Theirs is a world of thrilling outdoor adventures.

Fishing has always been one of the most popular activities that people enjoy. Many bodies of water—streams, rivers, lakes, and more—provide the opportunity to match wits with fish. And if you prefer your angling a little more extreme, deep-sea fishing may be for you. Technically, deep-sea fishing takes place in water more than 100 feet (30.5 m) deep, though typically you'll go into waters several times deeper than that. You'll also encounter many different types of fish, some of which are among the world's largest and weigh hundreds of pounds. Are you ready to cast off?

Fishing Then and Now

Fishing began many centuries ago, with evidence of people eating fish as part of their diets dating back to at least 40,000 B.C. It's likely that the first fishing tool was the gorge, a short piece of bone or wood sharpened at both ends and attached to a line. The gorge would be covered in bait. When a fish chomped on the bait, the fisherman would give a quick tug on the line, embedding the sharp points of the gorge in its mouth. Then he would simply pull on the line to bring his catch to shore.

t's not clear when hooks were developed, but archaeologists have discovered them in ancient Egypt, Rome, Greece, and other civilizations. Fishing rods—which were originally probably sticks or tree branches—and nets were used by such peoples as well. Though primitive, these early forms of fishing tackle were effective. A famous 3,500-year-old **fresco** from the Greek island of Santorini depicts a young man clutching

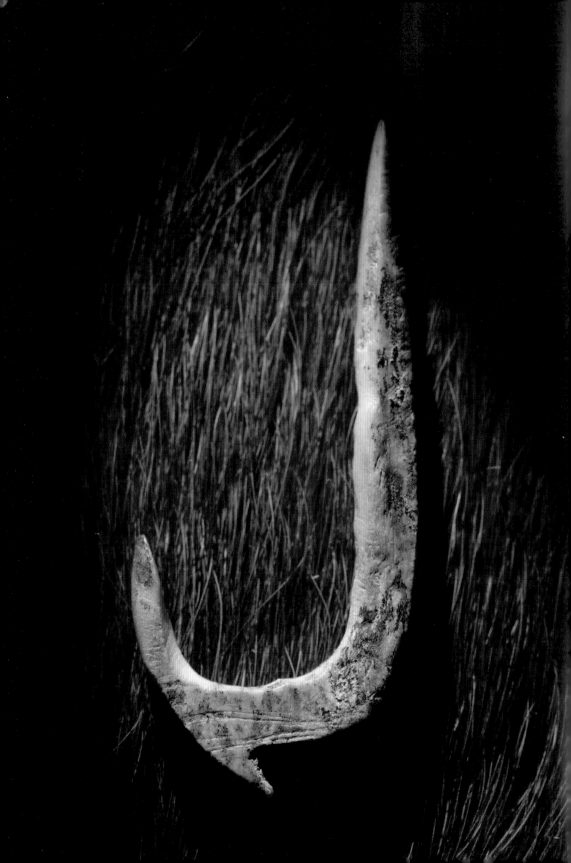

at least a dozen fish. Initially, hooks were made of wood or bone. After the invention of copper and bronze, they were among the first tools to be made using this new technology. The angular shape of the hook prompted fishing to become known as "angling." A key design development was the barb, a sharp projection near the tip of the hook that juts outward. The barb embedded the hook in the fish's mouth and kept the fish from spitting it out. New technology in the 16th and 17th centuries resulted in better rods and hooks as well as the development of the reel. Originally, the reel was simply a wooden spool with extra line coiled around it. This extra line made it easier to control the fish. The fisherman would allow his prey to swim away with the hook in its mouth. As the fish weakened, he would take in the line and finally bring the fish to him.

istorians aren't sure when fishing became a recreational activity. Egyptian and Chinese accounts suggest that it may date back more than 2,000 years. The first recorded mention of fishing as anything other than a source of food dates to the 1496 publication of an essay entitled "The Treatyse of Fyssynghe with an Angle." The author, Dame Juliana Berners, was an avid outdoorswoman who served as the prioress, or head, of a nunnery in England. Dame Juliana wrote about seasonal activities and topics, and many of her observations sound as if they could have been written today. Though the book was often reprinted, recreational fishing in that era was limited to the nobility. They feared that the common people could not exercise self-control in fishing and might "utterly destroye it."

About a century and a half later, what is probably the most famous fishing book of all time, Izaak Walton's *The Compleat Angler*, was published. It emphasized fishing simply for the sake of fishing and therefore as pure recreation. By this time, nobles weren't the only ones who were fishing. Walton included information on the feeding habits of a variety of fish and the best baits for catching them. "No life is so happy and so pleasant as the life of the well-govern'd angler," he wrote. Generations of anglers since then have echoed those words.

By the middle of the 19th century, construction of all types of tackle had vastly improved. The new materials also opened up recreational angling to many more people, though it's likely that nearly all of them were using lakes, rivers, and fishing in coastal waters while standing on the beach. Some authorities maintain that the sport of deep-sea fishing originated just off California's Santa Catalina Island when Dr. Charles Holder hauled in a 183-pound (83 kg) bluefin tuna on June 1, 1898. Soon afterward, he helped found the Tuna Club of Avalon, the world's first game fishing organization. It would serve as a model for many similar groups around the world.

Holder had used a rowboat. The invention of reliable motors and the corresponding rise in deep-sea sport fishing vessels in the succeeding decades made it possible to venture farther offshore, where the largest and fastest fish awaited eager anglers. The sheer variety of ocean fish, along with environmental variables such as tides, currents, weather, and even the phases of the moon, have created a multitude of challenges for anglers.

In recent decades, "catch and release" has become increasingly popular. That means that you still try to catch as many fish as possible. Rather than bringing them aboard and killing them, however, you remove the hook (preferably while the fish is still in the water), and allow them to return to their natural habitat. Using barbless hooks greatly simplifies the process and makes removal virtually painless for the fish. Catch and release has become a more sustainable form of recreation in light of the effects climate change and overfishing have had on many fish populations. Among some larger types of fish, such as the blue shark, you may end up catching the same fish you had released earlier in the day!

Unfortunately, "shark finning" has also increased in recent years. This refers to the practice of removing sharks' fins and then throwing the sharks back into the sea. The fins are used for shark fin soup and some types of traditional Asian medicine. Even though bowls of

Ancient Swordfishing

Among his other writings, the Greek historian Polybius (c. 200–118 B.C.) recorded an account of swordfishing in the Mediterranean Sea. "A number of men lie in wait, two each in small two-oared boats," he wrote. "In the boat one man rows, while the other stands on the **prow** holding a spear ... The boat rows up to it [the swordfish], and the man with the spear strikes it at close quarters, and then pulls the spear-shaft away, leaving the harpoon in the fish's body; for it is barbed and loosely fastened to the shaft on purpose, and has a long rope attached to it. They then slacken the rope for the wounded fish, until it is wearied out with its convulsive struggles ... But sometimes it happens that the man rowing is wounded, right through the boat, by the immense size of the animal's sword."

shark fin soup sell for as much as $100, the rise of living standards in countries such as China has made it possible for more people to afford the pricey soup. Another factor contributing to the continuation of the practice is the mistaken belief that shark fins contain valuable nutrients. Shark finning is especially cruel to the sharks, which are usually still alive when tossed back into the sea. Unable to swim normally, they either drown or fall prey to other predators. Finning has had a devastating effect on global shark populations, with estimates of up to 100 million fins taken annually.

Tackling the Process of Purchasing Tackle

One of the best ways to get involved in deep-sea fishing is to attend meetings of local fishing clubs. Most of them are very welcoming and many offer instructional sessions for beginners. Members can also give advice about the best places to shop for tackle. If there isn't a club in your area, you can browse the Internet to familiarize yourself with fishing

OPPOSITE: Depending on the type of fishing you are doing, you will need different gear. Because saltwater fish are typically larger than freshwater, saltwater fishing usually requires heavier, stronger gear.

terminology and types of equipment. You may also have friends or relatives who are experienced anglers and would be happy to share their knowledge and have you tag along on their next expedition.

When the time comes to get your own equipment, find a shop staffed by knowledgeable salespeople. Many of them spend their off-hours on the water themselves, and they will be able to help you make the best choices for the type of fishing you plan on doing—within your budget.

In general, the larger the fish you're trying to catch, the longer the rod you'll need.

It's likely that your first purchase will be a rod. Most are made of fiberglass or carbon fiber and range between 5 and 12 feet (1.5–3.7 m) in length. In general, the larger the fish you're trying to catch, the longer the rod you'll need. Rods are flexible and bend easily. Flexibility is often referred to as "rod action." There are three basic types of rod action: Fast-action rods bend primarily in the upper third. Medium-action rods bend from the middle to the tip. And slow-action rods bend in the upper two-thirds of the rod. Slow-action and medium-action rods are best for beginners. Rods have several "eyes," which are loops at regular intervals along the length. The line feeds out through those eyes and provides better control as you

play the fish. Most rods are designed to be taken apart into shorter sections. This makes it easier to transport and store your rod. A rod bag keeps the parts together and reduces the risk of damage.

Connected to the rod is the reel, which holds the fishing line. A crank mounted on the side of the reel allows the angler to pull in the line. Most reels have a drag system. This eases the pressure on the line to keep it from snapping after the fish takes the bait and tries to escape. Most fishing lines are either monofilament—

made from a single strand of plastic—or braided from man-made fibers. Monofilament line is cheaper, more abrasion-resistant, easier to knot, and has the ability to stretch. Braided line is more expensive and thinner, allowing you to get more line onto the reel. Because it doesn't stretch, it also provides better hook-setting power.

The line in turn is connected to the hook, with the size depending on the type of fish you hope to catch—the larger the fish, the larger the hook. The eye on top of the hook attaches it to the line. The shank is the long

What's in a Name?

Most people know William Shakespeare (1564–1616) as the English author of immortal plays such as *Romeo and Juliet*, *Hamlet*, and *Julius Caesar*. To fishermen, William Shakespeare (1869–1950) is the American inventor of the level-winding fishing reel. For many years, frustrated anglers had dealt with the common problem of tangled lines on reels. A recreational fisherman himself, Shakespeare invented his device in 1895. As he reeled in the line, a bracket automatically traveled back and forth along the width of the reel, distributing the line evenly and thereby avoiding tangles. He applied for a **patent** and founded the Shakespeare Fishing Company in 1897. The company soon added other types of tackle and became successful. In 1959, Shakespeare was elected to the National Sporting Goods Hall of Fame.

portion, which makes a 180-degree curve at the bottom and ends at the point. Extending outward from the point is the barb, which keeps the hook in place when the fish takes it. The barb does the same thing with human skin when people accidentally get snagged. The best way to extract a hook is to keep pushing it through the skin until the point emerges on the other side. Cut the barb off and then pull the rest of the hook back out. Ouch!

Today, many hooks are barbless, which improves the process of catch and release. If you want to fish this way and can't find a barbless hook, it's easy to eliminate the barb. Simply clamp down hard on it with a pair of pliers.

Whether your plan is to release your catch or bring it home for dinner, you will want a net. Most have short handles for better control. Try to get one with a soft mesh, as it is less likely to injure the fish. This is especially important if you plan on letting the fish go. If you do, the net allows you to restrict the fish's movements as you quickly extract the hook.

Y ou'll need a tackle box to hold dozens of small items. In addition to specific fishing gear such as hooks, sinkers, lures, and so forth, you will want to include other helpful supplies. They may include a knife, pliers (preferably with built-in wire cutters), a cloth to wipe off your hands after handling a fish, and a measuring device to make sure that your fish are within legal limits. You should add first-aid supplies as well. Most tackle boxes are constructed with several layers. Each layer is divided into smaller compartments to separate items and help you quickly find what you are looking for.

You may also want gloves. Neoprene gloves keep your hands warm even if cold seawater splashes on them. Some have fold-back thumbs and fingers to enable speedy baiting of your hook. Some thumbs also have a slit to give you a better feel for the line. To keep your feet dry and comfortable, waterproof footwear is

helpful. Non-skid soles help you keep a better grip on a heaving deck. Thick socks keep your feet warm. Wool is a better choice than cotton, since wool retains heat even when wet.

You may need a fishing license for the type of fishing you will be doing. Because of the dangers of overfishing, many licenses contain size limits and restrictions on the number of fish you can take.

There are two basic strategies in catching saltwater fish. Many anglers prefer to use some form of bait such as worms or smaller fish. Attached to the hook, bait is either cast out or simply dropped over the side. Then you settle down and wait for the fish to come to the bait. Lures, on the other hand, are continuously worked. The angler tries to mimic the motions of a real sea creature and thereby convince a game fish to bite down on the hook embedded in the lure. Many lures have two or three separate hooks, with each one often having two or even three points to increase the chances of a catch.

Known to put up a fight when hooked, bluefish are among the most popular recreational species along the eastern coast of the United States. These fish can be more than 3 feet (0.9 m) long and weigh more than 25 pounds (11.3 kg).

World Records and World Leaders

One thing that makes deep-sea fishing extreme is the ever-present possibility of bad weather. While no charter boat captain would willingly expose clients to danger, sometimes freak storms can blow up with little warning. Modern sport fishing boats are designed with the possibility of encountering rough weather, but as the fate of the ocean liner *Titanic* tragically illustrates, no vessel is "unsinkable."

Another is the vast array of game fish. At one extreme are species such as bass, cod, and snapper, which often weigh just a few pounds (though some types can be considerably heavier). In the middle range are some "superstars": several varieties of sailfish and marlin tip the scales at around 150–200 pounds (68–90.7 kg). Less spectacular but still popular are salmon. The largest of these is the chinook, which tops out at nearly 100 pounds (45.4 kg). Considerably larger are yellowfin tuna, at 300 to 400 pounds (136–181 kg), and the Pacific halibut, weighing up to 450 pounds (204 kg).

Then there are the "big boys" such as the swordfish (with a world record weight of 1,182 pounds, or 536 kg) and sharks such as the mako (which soars as high

"Hooking and releasing a large blue marlin qualifies for many anglers as sport fishing's greatest challenge, thrill, and accomplishment."

as 20 feet [6.1 m] when hooked and tops out at 1,221 pounds [554 kg]). In a poll conducted among charter captains and other experts by *Sport Fishing* magazine, the blue marlin was named the world's top game fish. "Hooking and releasing a large blue marlin qualifies for many anglers as sport fishing's greatest challenge, thrill, and accomplishment," the magazine reported. "Blues are caught in oceans around the world on live and dead baits and large **trolled** lures."

Many deep-sea fishermen go out every time hoping to land an especially heavy fish, perhaps even setting a world record. However, a 2014 study called for an end to this practice among endangered species. Of the 1,200 species for which the Florida-based International Game Fish Association (IGFA) maintains records, at least 85 are at risk. Rather than bringing an endangered fish to a land-based weighing station, which almost always results in its death, the researchers suggest changing the record measurement from weight to length and documenting it with a camera or smart phone. Then the fish could be released. "Few policy changes in the world can do so much for so many species for so little cost," the study maintains.

Not everyone agrees. According to David Schiffman, one of the study's authors, "Several anglers said they were opposed to protecting these species, one of which is so **depleted** that it just became the first species of shark protected by the U.S. Endangered Species Act, because it would stop them from going for IGFA world records."

Catching Sharks

According to reliable estimates, humans kill more than 100 million sharks every year. That figure is based on the number of recorded catches, but many people catch sharks without reporting it. Another aspect of the problem of declining shark populations is bycatch. This refers to when commercial boats seeking fish such as tuna or mackerel accidentally haul in other species such as sharks in their nets. There has also been a substantial increase in shark-fishing tournaments. Many of these began after the release of the movie *Jaws* in 1975. Anglers pose proudly beside their sharks dangling from an overhead beam. Because sharks generally reproduce just once a year and at much lower rates than other fish, they cannot keep up with the pace of repopulation necessary to maintain even their current numbers.

While they may not be concerned about world records, U.S. presidents have frequently found fishing to be a good form of relaxation. As Daniel Xu of Outdoorhub.com wrote, "No other sport enjoys as much popularity in the White House as fishing does. Just about every American president, from Washington to Obama, has at some point taken the time during their term to cast a line. It's a tradition so ingrained in the office that it has become practically expected, and many presidents take it up as a beneficial photo opportunity."

Perhaps the most notable fisher-president was Herbert Hoover, who was elected in 1928 and served one term. His love for fishing was so great that Hal Elliott Wert entitled his 2005 biography of the former chief executive *Hoover: The Fishing President.* In the book's foreword, retired senator Mark Hatfield wrote, "Herbert Hoover was never more at peace than when he was standing in an Oregon stream in search of rainbow trout or trolling off the coast of Florida for fighting fish. Public service was his vocation, but fishing was his **respite** from a hectic world."

President George H. W. Bush was especially enthusiastic. His home in Kennebunkport, Maine, provided ample opportunity to fish offshore during his term (1989–1993) and afterward. He established the Presidential Fishing Tournament in Florida in 1990 and has hosted it every year since then. One of his most memorable outings came in 2007 when he hosted Russian president Vladimir Putin. "Although initially startled by the idea of an 83-year-old former president driving the boat at

Despite being partially paralyzed by polio, president Franklin D. Roosevelt enjoyed fishing in the Bahamas and elsewhere while he was in office. A special rig in his boats helped him fish more comfortably.

top speed, Putin loved the ride. (His interpreter looked like he was about to fly out the back of the boat)," wrote Bush's son and then president George W. Bush. "Putin was the only one who caught anything."

Almost certainly the most famous deep-sea fishing non-president was American author Ernest Hemingway. Several of his novels feature fishing, and a collection of his writing about the sport—*Hemingway on Fishing*—was published in 2002. He learned to fish as a child at his family's summer home in Michigan, and

it remained a lifelong passion. Hemingway spent many years living in Key West, Florida, and near Havana, Cuba. There he was able to match wits with the large game fish of the Caribbean and Gulf of Mexico. In 1950, he helped establish the Hemingway International Billfishing Tournament, one of the world's oldest big-game fishing tournaments, in the waters near Havana. He won the tournament during its first three years.

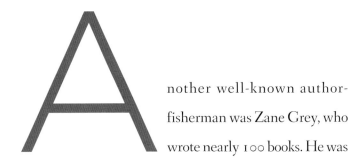

Another well-known author-fisherman was Zane Grey, who wrote nearly 100 books. He was most famous for his Western-themed novels, many of which were made into movies. They also served as the inspiration for two popular radio and TV series, *The Lone Ranger* and *Sergeant Preston of the Yukon*. His son estimated that the success of Grey's novels allowed him to spend up to 300 days fishing every year. At one time, he held 14 world records. "Zane Grey wrote to live and lived to fish," writes Marian Kester Coombs on the Zane Grey Collections website. "His articles on fishing were always anxiously anticipated by his readers, and when a Zane Grey fishing story came out, it usually sold out fast."

Fishing for Armchair Adventurers

Since fishing is such a popular activity, it's often the subject of books, films, and TV shows. The most famous book about deep-sea fishing is probably Ernest Hemingway's *The Old Man and the Sea*. Many high school, middle school, and even elementary school students read the book every year. Published in 1952, it is set in Cuba, where Hemingway lived for part of his life. The main character is an old

OPPOSITE: Actor Spencer Tracy played the title role in the 1958 film adaptation of *The Old Man and the Sea*, which was one of the earliest productions to make use of a special effect technique for layering two images together based on color hues (blue, in this case).

fisherman named Santiago. People in his village think he's unlucky because he hasn't caught anything for nearly three months. He has a young helper named Manolin. But Manolin's parents order the boy to leave Santiago and fish with more successful men. In an effort to change his luck, Santiago takes his boat far offshore and eventually hooks a huge marlin. It is so strong that it drags Santiago's boat for more than two days. Because Santiago can't let go of the line, his hands are raw and bleeding. He is exhausted from lack of sleep, but he does not give up. Finally, the marlin weakens. Santiago pulls him to the boat, lashes him to the side, and heads home. Sharks soon scent the dead marlin. Santiago tries to fight them off and kills several. But they keep coming. Eventually they eat most of the fish. Santiago reaches shore with the remains of the marlin and goes to his house, where he falls into a deep sleep. His fellow villagers are astonished by what he has caught. When Santiago wakes up, he and Manolin agree that they will fish together again. The book won the 1953 Pulitzer Prize for Fiction and was one of the main reasons why Hemingway also won the Nobel Prize in Literature the following year.

Hemingway also wrote *Islands in the Stream* (1970). The central character is a retired sculptor named Thomas Hudson (based on Hemingway himself), who settles on a remote Caribbean island. Part of the novel includes a deep-sea fishing trip with Hudson and his sons as they seek to land a giant marlin.

Carol Jean Tremblay plays on the widespread familiarity with Hemingway's work in her book for young people, *The Old Man and the C* (2006). Charley, the oldest fisherman in the region, has caught lots of little fish. But he's never hooked a big one. When the local bait and tackle shop announces the first-ever Fish-or-Cut Bait Tournament and offers a prize for the biggest fish, Charley hopes that his luck will change. He fires up the motor on his little boat, the *C-Worthy*, and chugs out to sea. When everyone else heads south, Charley turns the *C-Worthy* in the opposite direction. He baits his hook and drops it over the side. The adventure that follows resembles Hemingway's classic story—but with a twist at the end.

Jake Maddox, who has written about a variety of sports and outdoor activities for young readers, turns to fishing with *Legend of the Lure* (2009). Daniel spends many wonderful hours fishing with his grandfather, who helps pass the time with stories about his fishing achievements. But there's one thing his grandfather has never been able to do: catch the legendary fish nicknamed "Big Larry." After his grandfather dies, Daniel enters a tournament. His goal is to catch Big Larry and honor his grandfather's memory.

The annual run of coho salmon off the coast of Canada's Vancouver Island provides the background for Arthur Mayse's *Handliner's Island* (1990). Thirteen-year-old Paddy Logan spends his summer vacation learning how to **handline**. He wants to use the technique to catch enough fish so that the bank won't **foreclose** on his grandfather's island ranch. Besides the difficulties he encounters in learning how to handline, a group of robbers threatens him and his friend George when they set up camp on a tiny island. A local girl named Lynn helps the boys with their techniques, but it may not be enough.

Moviegoers can find plenty of fishing-related films. The first version of *The Old Man and the Sea* starred Spencer Tracy as Santiago. Some critics complain that much of the 1958 film was shot in a large tank rather than the open ocean. Two other versions of the story appeared: a 1990 TV mini-series starring Anthony Quinn, and a 20-minute 1999 animated short film that won an Academy Award. Hemingway's *Islands in the Stream* was also made into a film in 1977, starring George C. Scott.

A number of other noteworthy films were based on fishing-themed books. Many people classify *Jaws* (1975) as a fishing film, since the object is to catch the great white shark that terrorizes a New England beach town. Its inspiration was Peter Benchley's novel *Jaws*,

published a year earlier. While the shark is the "bad guy" in both versions, that wasn't always the case. "The film's director Steven Spielberg has admitted that when he first read the book he found most of the characters unlikeable, and wanted the shark to win," according to BBC News. And Benchley later said, "[T]he shark in an updated *Jaws* could not be the villain; it would have to be written as the victim; for, worldwide, sharks are much more the oppressed than the oppressors."

Yann Martel's 2001 fantasy novel *Life of Pi* centers on Piscine Molitor "Pi" Patel, the sole human survivor of a shipwreck during a violent storm in the Pacific Ocean. His "shipmate" on a lifeboat for more than 7 months is a Bengal tiger named Richard Parker. Pi learns to fish out of necessity. The book became a movie in 2012 and was nominated for 11 Academy Awards, winning 4.

The Perfect Storm

Published in 1997, Sebastian Junger's book *The Perfect Storm* was a bestseller. It centered on the 1991 loss of the fishing vessel *Andrea Gail* in the Atlantic Ocean during a severe storm. Three years later, the book was made into a movie, with George Clooney starring as the boat's captain Billy Tyne. The film opens with the vessel returning to port in Gloucester, Massachusetts, with yet another poor catch. Increasingly desperate for money, Tyne and his crew head back out to sea. After netting a good catch of swordfish, the vessel is caught in a severe storm. A massive wave capsizes the *Andrea Gail* and kills everyone on board. The film was successful at the box office and received two Academy Award nominations.

The U.S. Bureau of Labor Statistics rates commercial deep-sea fishing as the country's riskiest job.

The Discovery Channel debuted the series *Deadliest Catch* in 2005, and its 12th season began in March 2016. While it's filmed aboard vessels that catch crabs, the type of work and the accompanying dangers are similar to what any fishing boat encounters in the often-stormy Alaskan waters. The U.S. Bureau of Labor Statistics rates commercial deep-sea fishing as the country's riskiest job in terms of the chance of death. Viewers can understand why as they watch the crews in action on the high seas.

A Day on the Water

Some people are fortunate enough to own a boat suitable for deep-sea fishing. However, most people pursue the sport by going out on a charter boat. These boats can be less than 30 feet (9.1 m) to more than 50 feet (15.2 m) long. They typically charge between $30 and $100, depending on how long the trip lasts. You can bring your own tackle or rent it. If you're just starting out, it's probably better to rent. The crew will know the best type

OPPOSITE: Some of the best times to fish are early in the morning, near sunrise, and around sunset in the evening. Fish often feed in the mornings and evenings, so they are more likely to strike at an angler's bait during these times.

of tackle for where you're headed.

Fishing from a charter boat has several advantages. The skippers and crew know the best places to go for fish and the best seasons for particular fish. They are also adept at reading signs. For example, if a flock of seagulls or other seabirds is hovering over a certain spot on the water, it's likely that they have their eyes on fish small enough for them to catch. And where there are small fish, it's a strong possibility that larger ones are lurking nearby. Reefs are another possible source. Many smaller fish make their homes there, and that in turn attracts their larger cousins. Charter boat personnel are also familiar with licensing requirements and can help with preparing tackle and baiting hooks.

The number of anglers varies with the size of the boat, from a relative handful to 20 or more. Many fill

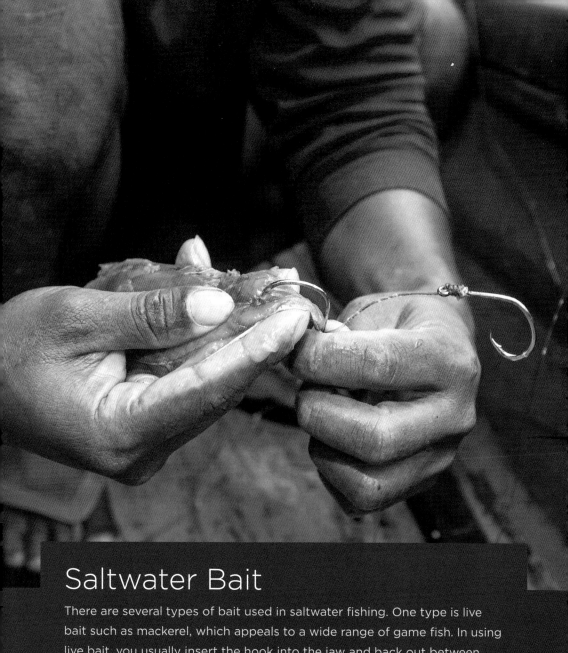

Saltwater Bait

There are several types of bait used in saltwater fishing. One type is live bait such as mackerel, which appeals to a wide range of game fish. In using live bait, you usually insert the hook into the jaw and back out between the eyes. That's because fish generally strike at the head of their prey. Another form of bait is crustaceans (crabs, shrimp, etc.). Fish especially like "peelers," or crabs that are about to molt and shed their shells. Anglers may also use whole or parts of dead fish as bait. And worms are in common use. Bait is often frozen, and then thawed shortly before use. It's not a good idea to keep thawing and refreezing the same bait because it loses more of its scent each time, becoming less appealing to fish.

up quickly, so making reservations as far in advance as possible is recommended. In some cases, you can charter the entire boat for your own party. In general, every angler is allotted a couple feet of space along the railing. Some boats that specialize in large game fish may have just a single "fighting chair," mounted on a swivel near the stern, or the back of the boat. The end of the rod fits into a large tube next to the chair.

The crew members will be happy to answer questions if they have time. But chances are they will be

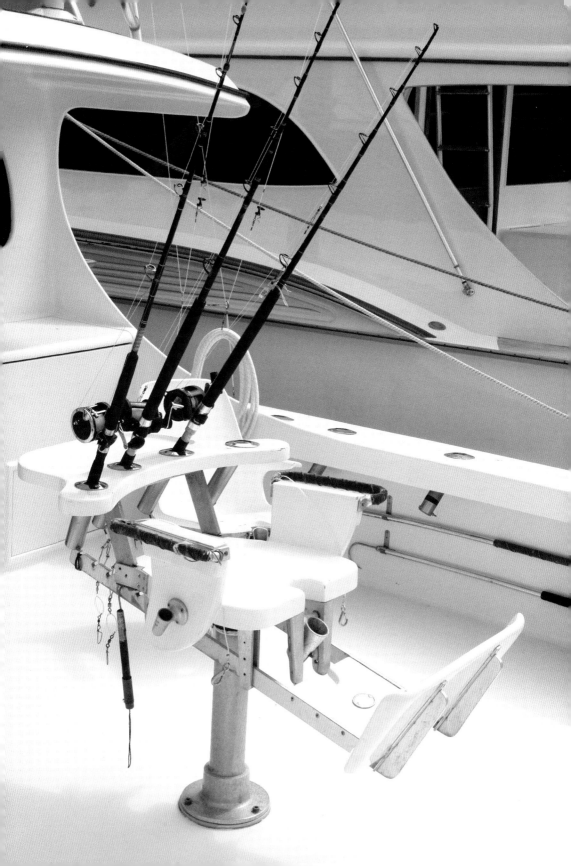

Conditions at sea can change without warning, so it is best to wear layers.

busy from the time you cast off until you arrive at the fishing site. Therefore, before your trip, it's a good idea to familiarize yourself as much as possible with the area where you will be fishing and the types of fish you're likely to encounter.

One important consideration as you plan your trip is the possibility of becoming seasick. Occasionally you'll be on water that is flat and calm. However, your boat will likely bob up and down in the swells. Consider taking an over-the-counter medication such as Dramamine® to prevent motion sickness. Be sure to take it before you leave shore, as it's probably too late to be effective once you start feeling nauseous.

Conditions at sea can change without warning, so it is best to wear layers. You can take off clothing and put it back on to match the conditions you encounter. Temperatures can be as much as 20 degrees cooler at sea than on land. Also, the forward motion of the boat creates wind, so wearing a hoodie or windbreaker is a good idea. Rain boots or other footwear with non-slip soles are best. For protection from the sun, bring sunblock, sunglasses, and a hat. Some like baseball caps, while others prefer headgear with wider brims. Binoculars add to your enjoyment. And don't forget a camera!

As soon as you come on board, find a place to safely stow your gear. As the boat casts off, the skipper is likely to come on the intercom with information about overall safety, the specific locations of life jackets, and the conditions to expect. The run out to your destination is likely to take at least half an hour. During that time, the crew will be getting everything ready.

When you reach the fishing ground, find an open spot along the railing with your tackle, and wait for the captain to announce that it's time to put your line into the water. If you drop your line while the boat is still moving, there's a good chance you'll get tangled with someone else or with the propeller. Be considerate of your neighbors. If

you're using live bait, wait until this time to bait your hook.

You're likely to spend several hours at the site, so be sure to reel in your line if you need to take a break. When you put it back in, replace the bait. Even if you're not taking a break, frequently changing your bait is a good idea. The key appeal of bait is its scent, which attracts fish from far away, and bait loses its scent fairly quickly. It should be kept cool until it's needed to prevent it from spoiling. Hopefully, you'll have the thrill of catching at least one fish before it's time to head back. The charter's crew members will go to work cleaning and slicing the day's catch. For a modest fee (usually a dollar or two per fish), they will make it table-ready for you. Unless you're experienced, letting them do this dirty work is a good idea. It's also a good idea to tip your crew, even if you don't catch anything. You would expect to tip a waiter

at a restaurant, and crew members often work under considerably more trying conditions.

A s the boat ties up and you step onto the dock, you're likely to be tired but happy. There are few things that compare with the almost electric sensation when you feel an invisible fish at the end of your line. And when you bring it alongside and actually get to see it close up—whether you choose to keep it or let it go—you have the satisfaction of the ultimate fishing experience.

Glossary

depleted   reduced to very low levels

foreclose   to take over a property because of failures to meet mortgage payments

fresco   watercolor painting done on wet plaster, which allows the colors to penetrate the plaster and become fixed as it dries

handline   a fishing technique in which a person holds a single line in his or her hands

lures   types of bait made of wood, plastic, or metal

neoprene   an oil-resistant synthetic (man-made) rubber, characterized by flexibility, abrasion resistance, and insulating properties

patent   a government license that protects an inventor's right to make and sell an invention without competition for a set period

prow   the front of a boat

respite   a short period of rest or relief from doing something difficult or unpleasant

sinkers   balls made of metal that pull the hook down in the water

trolled   trailed a baited line behind a slowly moving boat

Selected Bibliography

Bailey, John. *Fishing*. New York: Dorling Kindersley, 2001.

Bailey, John, Peter Gathercole, Trevor Housby, Dennis Moss, Bruce Vaughan, and Phil Williams. *The New Encyclopedia of Fishing*. New York: Dorling Kindersley, 2001.

Freda, Jim, Gene Quigley, and Shell E. Caris. *Saltwater Fishing: A Tactical Approach*. Short Hills, N.J.: Burford Books, 2004.

Gilbey, Henry. *The Complete Fishing Manual*. New York: Dorling Kindersley, 2011.

Mojetta, Angelo, ed. *Simon & Schuster's Guide to Saltwater Fish and Fishing*. New York: Simon & Schuster, 1992.

Pollizotto, Martin. *Saltwater Fishing Made Easy*. Camden, Maine: McGraw-Hill, 2006.

Ristori, Al. *Complete Guide to Saltwater Fishing*. Upper Saddle River, N.J.: Creative Outdoors, 2004.

Schaffner, Herbert A. *Saltwater Game Fish of North America*. New York: Gallery Books, 1990.

Websites

International Game Fish Association
https://www.igfa.org

The official IGFA site contains historic videos, international fishing rules, news, features, a list of world records for more than 1,200 fish, and more.

Saltwater Fishing Tackle and Accessories
http://saltfishing.about.com/od/tackleandaccessories/

This website has hundreds of detailed articles covering every aspect of saltwater fishing and links to even more.

Note: Every effort has been made to ensure that any websites listed above were active at the time of publication. However, because of the nature of the Internet, it is impossible to guarantee that these sites will remain active indefinitely or that their contents will not be altered.

Index